The Battle of Yorktown

The Battle of Yorktown

Dennis Brindell Fradin

Marshall Cavendish Benchmark
New York

Marshall Cavendish Benchmark
99 White Plains Road
Tarrytown, New York 10591-5502
www.marshallcavendish.us

Maps by XNR Productions

All Internet sites were available and accurate when sent to press.

Library of Congress Cataloging-in-Publication Data
Fradin, Dennis B.
The Battle of Yorktown / by Dennis Brindell Fradin.
p. cm. — (Turning points in U.S. history)
Includes bibliographical references and index.
ISBN 978-0-7614-3008-7
1. Yorktown (Va.)—History—Siege, 1781—Juvenile literature. I. Title.
E241.Y6F73 2008
973.3'37—dc22
2007030450

Photo research by Connie Gardner

Cover photo by The Granger Collection
Cover Photo: An oil painting by N.C. Wyeth depicts George Washington overseeing the Battle of Yorktown.
Title Page: American troops capture a British stronghold at the Battle of Yorktown in Virginia.

The photographs in this book are used by permission and through the courtesy of: *The Granger Collection:* 3, 18, 26, 28; *NorthWind Picture Archives:* 6, 10, 14, 17, 20, 24, 31, 33, 35, 36, 42-43; *Corbis:* Bettmann, 8; *Art Resource:* Reunion des Musees Nationaux, 22.

Editor: Deborah Grahame
Publisher: Michelle Bisson
Art Director: Anahid Hamparian

Printed in Malaysia
1 3 5 6 4 2

Contents

Protestors of the Stamp Act are shown building a bonfire to destroy a tax official's carriage.

CHAPTER ONE

England's Thirteen Colonies Rebel

Between 1607 and 1733, England settled or seized control of thirteen **colonies** in North America. The colonists had few complaints about British rule until the 1760s. Then trouble broke out over taxes.

Britain passed the Stamp Act in 1765. According to this law, Americans had to buy special tax stamps. The stamps were to be placed on newspapers, legal **documents**, and other paper goods. The Stamp Act sparked **protests** and even **riots** across the thirteen colonies. The Tea Act of 1773 caused similar trouble. Instead of paying this tax, Americans threw British tea into the ocean. The most famous such protest was the Boston Tea Party of December 16, 1773.

At the Boston Tea Party in 1773, about 150 men, some dressed as Indians, dumped more than three hundred chests of British tea into Boston Harbor.

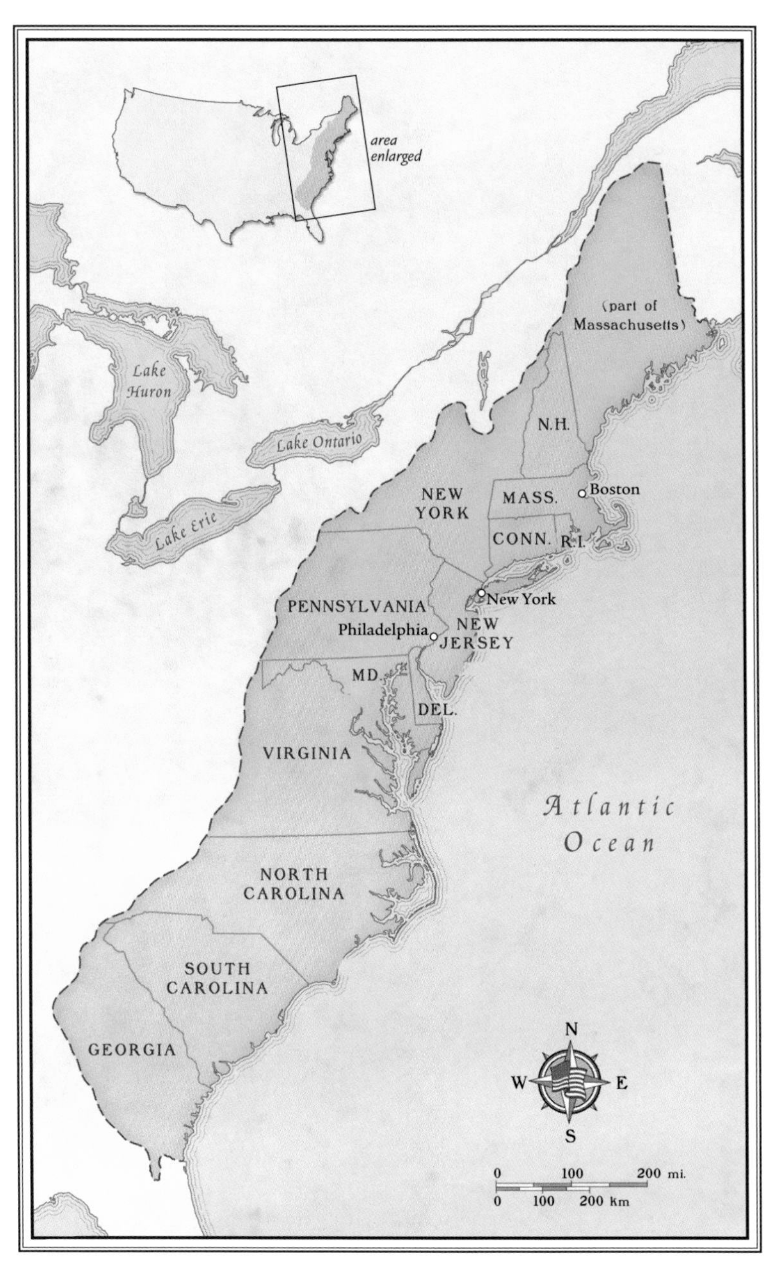

The original thirteen American colonies

King George III and other British leaders were determined to stop the **rebellion.** They sent troops across the ocean to keep watch on the colonists. In fall 1774 American leaders met in Philadelphia, Pennsylvania, to decide what to do. Their meeting became known as the First Continental Congress. The leaders told all thirteen colonies to make sure their **militias** were ready to fight. The soldiers would have to act quickly if war broke out with Britain.

The Boston Massacre was a turning point in the conflict between Britain and the colonies, helping to ignite the Revolutionary War.

CHAPTER TWO

The Revolutionary War Begins

Everyone knew where the war was most likely to start. Boston, Massachusetts, was the most rebellious American town. The most violent protests against the Stamp Act had occurred there. In 1770 British troops had shot and killed five men at a brawl called the Boston Massacre. Bostonians had also held the most **notorious** tea party.

In spring 1775 the British planned a double attack on the rebels in the Boston area. An army of redcoats (British soldiers) would march out of Boston. They would capture the rebel leaders Samuel Adams and John Hancock, who were hiding in nearby Lexington, Massachusetts. The

This map highlights important locations and events in the colonists' struggle for independence.

redcoats would then continue a few miles to Concord, where they would **seize** some of the colonists' military supplies.

Rebels in Boston discovered the British plan. They sent Paul Revere to Lexington on horseback. Thanks to Revere's warning, Adams and Hancock escaped before the redcoats arrived, and Lexington's militiamen prepared to fight.

The redcoats reached Lexington at dawn on April 19, 1775. The Lexington militiamen fought them, but they were defeated. Later that day, though, the Americans won the Battle of Concord. The clashes at Lexington and Concord began the war for American **independence**.

Under an elm tree that still stands today, General George Washington took command of the Continental Army against Britain in 1775.

CHAPTER THREE

The Americans Take a Pounding

Less than a month after the war began, the Second Continental Congress began in Philadelphia. In June 1775 the congress formed a national army. It was called the Continental Army. George Washington of Virginia was chosen as its commander in chief.

In 1776 another Virginian, Thomas Jefferson, wrote the Declaration of Independence. This paper announced that Britain's thirteen colonies had become the United States of America. Americans still celebrate the day Congress issued the Declaration of Independence—July 4, 1776—as their nation's birthday.

"Father" Washington

George Washington was born in Westmoreland County, Virginia. Before he turned twelve, his father and one of his sisters died. Young Washington went to work as a **surveyor**. At age seventeen, he helped lay out streets for the new town of Alexandria, Virginia.

Like many other American colonists, Washington helped Britain fight the French and Indian War. "I luckily escaped without a wound, though I had four bullets through my coat and two horses shot under me," he wrote about a battle he fought in 1755.

Twenty years later, Washington was chosen to lead the Continental Army against Britain. For most of the war, Americans criticized Washington for avoiding big battles. He knew that a big battle might destroy his army. Only after Yorktown did Washington become a national hero.

George Washington (1732–1799)

Declaring independence was the easy part. Actually winning it was another story. England, the world's most powerful nation, had many advantages over the Americans on the battlefield.

To start with, the British army was larger. At top strength, England's army in America totaled 50,000 men. Washington's largest revolutionary army had just 20,000 men.

The redcoats were well trained. The American troops had little training, especially early in the war. Even worse, the Continental Congress did not have enough funds to meet its army's needs. American soldiers often went hungry. They had to raid beehives and pick berries to keep from starving. In addition, General Washington had to schedule battles around certain dates. This was because most American soldiers signed up for short periods of time.

As a result, things looked bleak for the Americans for the first few years of the war. It often seemed like the stroke of midnight was at hand, and the United States would turn back into the thirteen colonies.

The Americans suffered defeat after defeat. For example, the four largest American cities during revolutionary times were Philadelphia (40,000 people), New York (25,000), Boston (16,000), and Charleston, South Carolina (12,000). All four cities fell to the enemy.

A low point for the Americans came in late 1777. A few days before Christmas, General Washington marched his remaining army—11,000

Washington is shown visiting troops in Valley Forge. The soldiers gained military skills during the harsh six months they spent there.

men—to winter quarters at Valley Forge, Pennsylvania. On their way into Valley Forge, the soldiers left bloody footprints on the frozen ground. Half the troops no longer had shoes. The winter at Valley Forge was terrible. More than three thousand men died from cold, hunger, and disease.

General Washington was not a man who gave up easily. However, even he felt the cause was nearly hopeless. On December 23, 1777, he wrote to the Continental Congress from Valley Forge. "Unless some great and capital change suddenly takes place," Washington predicted, "this Army must be **inevitably** reduced to one of three things: starve, **dissolve**, or **disperse**."

Benjamin Franklin convinced King Louis XVI of the advantage of a French alliance with American forces during the Revolutionary War.

CHAPTER FOUR

Good News from France

In spring 1778 wonderful news arrived from Europe. This was the "great and capital change" Washington needed. Thanks largely to Benjamin Franklin's work as a **diplomat**, France entered the war on the American side.

French soldiers and sailors were a great help to the Americans. Their weapons, ships, and money helped, too. In June 1778 the British fled Philadelphia because a large French **fleet** was on the way. Yet the years 1778, 1779, and 1780 passed, and still the Americans could not deal the redcoats a crushing blow. That opportunity finally came in 1781.

"Papa Rochambeau"

Jean-Baptiste Donatien de Vimeur, Comte (Count) de Rochambeau, was born in Vendôme, France. Rochambeau studied to become a priest, but his life took a sharp turn in another direction. For centuries at least one member of his family had served in the French army. An older brother of Rochambeau's was carrying out that role, but he died. Rochambeau then left his religious studies and entered a military academy. He was a soldier by the age of seventeen and a general by his early thirties.

Rochambeau showed great concern for his troops. His men called him Papa Rochambeau. George Washington called Rochambeau his "fellow laborer in the cause of liberty." The two leaders became friends. Together they made plans that led to victory at Yorktown—and independence for the Americans.

In 1783 Rochambeau returned to France. He lived to the age of eighty-one.

Jean-Baptiste Donatien de Vimeur (1725–1807)

On May 22 an important meeting was held in Wethersfield, Connecticut. General Washington met with General Rochambeau, commander of the French forces in America. Washington and Rochambeau agreed that their combined forces were strong enough to make a major attack on the British. One big question remained: Where?

Washington had a strong preference. After the British drove his troops out of New York City in 1776, he became determined to recapture it.

Washington and Rochambeau chose New York City as their target. They would have to overcome General Henry Clinton, commander of British forces in America, and his ten thousand troops. Defeating such a huge force might win the war for the Americans.

Over the next few months, however, the situation changed. Washington learned that a large British army was taking up quarters in the little tobacco port of Yorktown, Virginia. The army's leader, General Charles Cornwallis, had vowed to crush America at his feet. There was more news. A large French fleet, under Admiral Count François de Grasse, was headed to Chesapeake Bay, near Yorktown.

The new information changed everything. Victory would be easier in Yorktown than it would be in New York City. The combined American and French troops could close in on the enemy by land. Meanwhile, Admiral de Grasse's ships could block the redcoats' escape by sea. Washington changed his mind. Yorktown, Virginia, would be the target.

Rochambeau, shown on the left greeting Washington, had far more military experience than the American general.

CHAPTER FIVE

On to Yorktown

General Rochambeau put himself and his troops under General Washington's command. In August 1781 Washington led the American–French army on its journey south. They started out in what is now New York State. Over a few weeks they passed through parts of New Jersey, Pennsylvania, Delaware, Maryland, and Virginia. After a 450-mile (724-kilometer) march, the soldiers arrived at Yorktown in late September.

The scene was set for a tremendous fight. Cornwallis's army had taken up positions in and near Yorktown. They had dug trenches and built **fortifications** and gun platforms. The Americans did the same outside

Charles Cornwallis

Charles Cornwallis was born in London, England, on New Year's Eve of 1738. He attended Eton, a school outside London, where one of his eyes was injured in a hockey game. Cornwallis became a lawmaker and a soldier. He received the title Earl Cornwallis in 1762. He was sent to America to command British troops in the clash with the rebels.

General Cornwallis won many battles, and people considered him a fine general. Why, then, did he get trapped in Yorktown? Some people blamed General Clinton for not sending help in time. Others blamed Cornwallis for leading his army into a poor position. Perhaps it was both of their faults. The two men disliked each other, and communication between them was poor.

Cornwallis later commanded British forces in India and Ireland. He died in India in 1805 at the age of sixty-six.

Charles Cornwallis
(1738–1805)

Yorktown. Meanwhile, Admiral de Grasse's large fleet blocked the British from getting away by sea.

Both sides had plenty of artillery—cannons and other big guns—at Yorktown. The British had sixty-five artillery pieces. However, Washington's army had 124—almost twice as many. The British had 7,500 troops. With nearly 20,000 men, the American–French force was nearly triple that size. Washington's troops had been defeated numerous times earlier in the war. This time they were ready to strike hard at the enemy.

General Washington fires a cannon. Several buildings in Yorktown, Virginia, survived the battle and can be seen today.

CHAPTER SIX

The Battle of Yorktown

After a few minor fights, serious warfare began on October 9, 1781. On that day Washington's troops began firing their artillery at the British from outside Yorktown. Joseph Plumb Martin, a soldier from Connecticut, described the Americans' opening **bombardment**:

> *I felt a secret pride swell my heart when I saw the "star-spangled banner" waving majestically in the very faces of our* ***adversaries.*** *A discharge of all the guns in the line followed. It was said that the first shell entered an elegant house [occupied by] a large party of British officers at dinner, killing and wounding a number of them.*

There was some close-up fighting at the Battle of Yorktown. For example, General Washington wanted to capture two British outposts. French troops attacked one. An American party led by Colonel Alexander Hamilton attacked the other. Both outposts were taken, and a large number of British soldiers were killed or captured.

The Battle of Yorktown was largely an artillery fight, however. As they fired their big guns at each other, both sides suffered **casualties**. Even the commanders had close calls. Once, when General Washington was out observing the battlefield, an enemy cannonball landed close to him. General Cornwallis was in a trench when a cannonball suddenly zoomed by. The ball hit a British officer, and his headless body fell at Cornwallis's feet.

Having more troops, weapons, and **ammunition** made a huge difference. The Americans and the French pounded the British defenses until the ground at Yorktown looked like the craters of the moon. James Thacher, an American army doctor, later said that the ground trembled from the firing of the big guns. Dr. Thacher added:

> *All around was thunder and lightning from our numerous cannon and mortars. . . . Some of our shells, overreaching the town, are seen to fall into the river, and bursting, throw up columns of water, like the spouting of the monsters of the deep.*

After several days of bombardment, two important British outposts gave way to American and French troops.

Johann Conrad Doehla, a German soldier fighting on the British side, described what it was like on the receiving end of the attack:

> *The bombs and cannon balls hit many inhabitants of [Yorktown], and marines, soldiers, and sailors. One saw men lying nearly everywhere who were mortally wounded and whose heads, arms, and legs had been shot off. . . . I saw bombs fall into the water and lie there for 5, 6, 8 and more minutes and then still explode. . . . The fragments and pieces of the bombs . . . robbed many a brave soldier of his life or struck off an arm or leg.*

General Cornwallis had one hope. Under cover of darkness, letters were sent in and out of Yorktown in small boats. Cornwallis informed General Clinton up in New York about his desperate situation. Clinton replied that he was sending twenty-three warships with about five thousand British

An International Battle

The Battle of Yorktown did not just involve British, American, and French troops. Men from several other countries were also involved. The British side included large numbers of men from Germany. The American–French forces included men from Canada, Germany, Sweden, and Poland.

The French used hot-shot, cannonballs heated red-hot, to destroy the British ship *Charon* during the battle.

troops to Yorktown. This fleet was expected to arrive around mid-October. If Cornwallis could hold out until then, he might win the battle.

By October 12 the British troops were aboard the warships and ready to leave New York. The next day, just before the ships were supposed to set sail, a huge storm hit New York harbor. The storm delayed the fleet's departure by a few **crucial** days.

Meanwhile, at Yorktown the British were still taking a beating. On October 17 the Americans and the French began their biggest **barrage** yet. A hundred artillery pieces were now pounding the British forces. With no sign of the fleet from New York, Cornwallis knew that the battle was lost. That morning, he sent a letter of **surrender** to General Washington:

York, Virginia 17th Octr. 1781

Sir

I propose a ***cessation*** *of hostilities for twenty four hours, and that two officers may be appointed by each side to meet at Mr. Moore's house to settle terms for the surrender of the posts of York and Gloucester. I have the honour to be*

Sir

Your most obedient and most humble servant

Cornwallis

His Excellency
General Washington

British drums beat steadily, announcing the wish to parley, or discuss terms of surrender.

A British officer hands over Cornwallis's sword to an American officer. During the battle, more than five hundred British soldiers had been killed, wounded, or were missing.

Washington quickly answered Cornwallis. He wrote that he wanted to stop "the further [spilling] of Blood." Washington stopped attacking while the two sides worked out the details of the British surrender. More letters were exchanged, and meetings were held. It was agreed that Cornwallis's army would surrender on October 19, 1781.

On that Friday afternoon, the British surrendered a huge army—more than seven thousand men. Washington's troops were polite at the surrender ceremony. Once the British were marched off under guard, though, the American soldiers began to celebrate. An American officer described the scene:

> *I noticed that the officers and soldiers could scarcely talk for laughing and they could scarcely stand for jumping and dancing and singing. . . .*

The Americans suspected that they had won more than a battle. They hoped their victory at Yorktown might end the war.

In late October the rescue fleet from New York finally arrived to assist the British at Yorktown. It was too late. General Cornwallis had surrendered several days earlier.

Meanwhile, word of the victory at Yorktown was spreading throughout America. In Philadelphia, the new nation's capital, a messenger rode

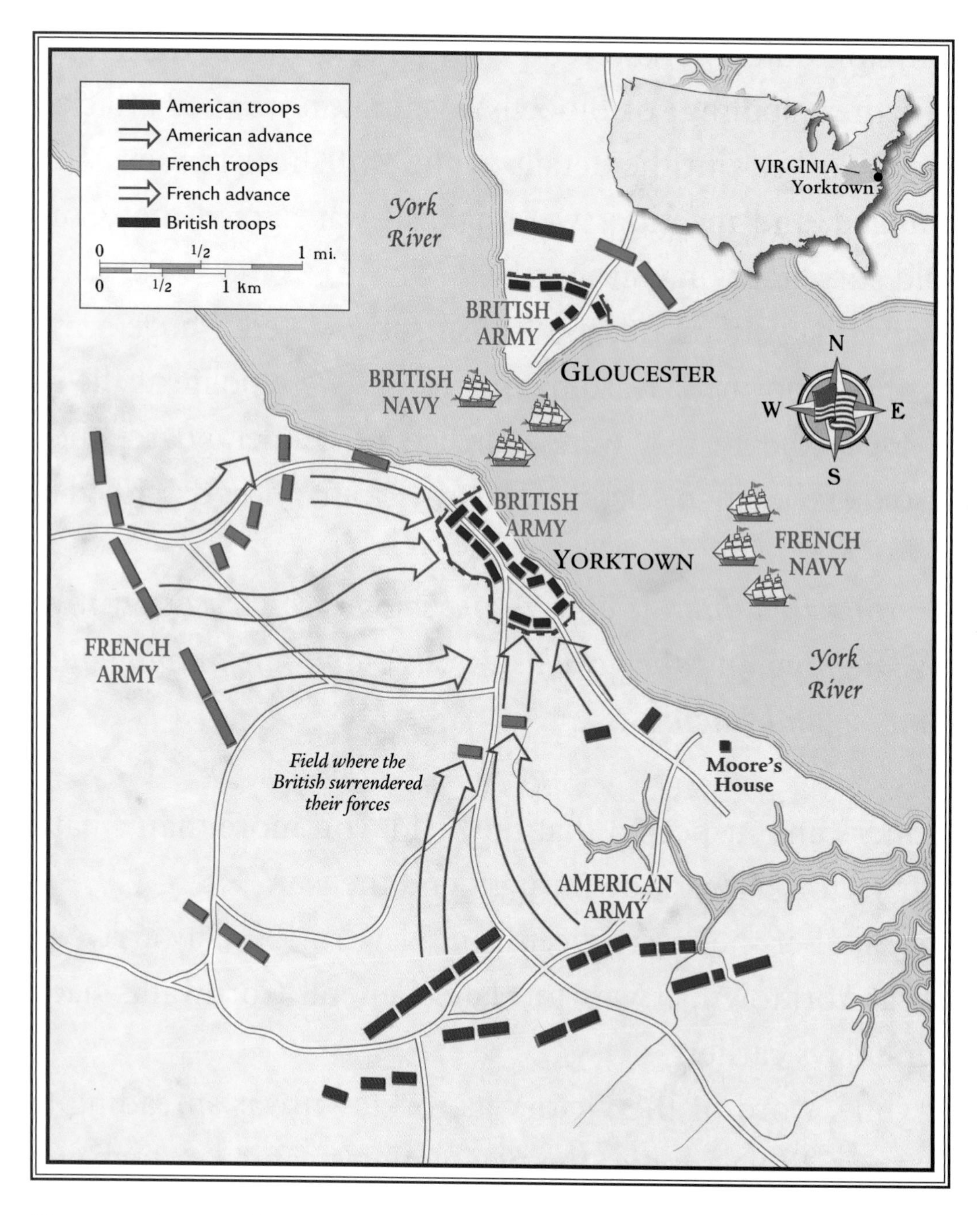

This map shows military movements at the Battle of Yorktown.

into town yelling, “Great news! Cornwallis is taken!” Soon the bells of Independence Hall were ringing out the joyous news. The Declaration of Independence had been issued in this building five years earlier.

The American and the French troops’ victory at Yorktown was the turning point of the Revolutionary War. In fact it was the war’s last major battle. After their crushing defeat at Yorktown, the British did not want to continue the fight.

On September 3, 1783, Britain and America signed a peace **treaty**. The signing took place in Paris, France. This was a fitting site because the French had helped the Americans win the war. With this agreement the Revolutionary War ended. A new country, the United States of America, took its place among the nations of the world.

Glossary

adversaries—People or groups that are fighting each other.

ammunition—Bullets, cannonballs, and other materials that are fired from weapons.

barrage—A heavy firing of weapons.

bombardment—An attack using bombs, cannons, or other large weapons.

casualties—Deaths or injured soldiers in a battle.

cessation—A stoppage (sometimes temporary).

colonies—Settlements built by a country beyond its borders.

crucial—Very important.

diplomat—Someone who works to cooperate with a foreign country.

disperse—To break up or scatter.

dissolve—To disappear; to fade away.
documents—Important official papers.
fleet—A group of ships often traveling together.
fortifications—Structures that support a military position.
independence—Freedom or self-government.
inevitably—Definitely; without doubt.
militias—Groups of regular citizens organized for military service.
notorious—Widely known, usually for being dangerous or evil.
protests—Objections; acts against authority.
rebellion—An attempt to break free of authority.
riots—Violent demonstrations in public.
seize—To take; to steal.
surrender—An admission of defeat by an enemy.
surveyor—A person who figures out land boundaries.
treaty—An official agreement between countries or organizations.

Timeline

1607—The English settle Virginia, the first of Britain's thirteen American colonies

1754–1763—With the American colonists' help, Britain wins the French and Indian War

1765—Americans rebel against Britain's Stamp Act tax

1773—The Boston Tea Party is held to protest Britain's Tea Act

1774—September 5: The First Continental Congress, a meeting of American colonial leaders, opens in Philadelphia

1775—April 19: The Revolutionary War begins in Massachusetts at Lexington and Concord
May 10: The Second Continental Congress opens in Philadelphia

1776—July 4: The Declaration of Independence is issued

1607 *1773* *1776*

1777–1778—George Washington's American army spends a disastrous winter at Valley Forge, Pennsylvania

1778—France enters the war on the American side

1781—September 28: Combined American and French forces arrive at Yorktown
October 9: George Washington's forces begin bombarding British troops
October 19: The British surrender at Yorktown

1783—By the Treaty of Paris, Britain recognizes Americans' independence

2006—Americans celebrate the 225th anniversary of the Battle of Yorktown

1781

1783

2006

Further Information

BOOKS

Anderson, Dale. *The Battle of Yorktown*. New York: Gareth Stevens, 2004.

DK Publishing. *American Revolution* (Eyewitness Books). New York: Dorling Kindersley, 2005.

Ingram, Scott. *The Battle of Yorktown*. San Diego: Blackbirch Press, 2003.

Vierow, Wendy. *The Battle of Yorktown*. New York: Rosen, 2003.

WEB SITES

This is the home page of Colonial National Historical Park, which includes Yorktown Battlefield:
www.nps.gov/colo

This site provides an overview of the Battle of Yorktown, as well as the surrender agreement:
www.battleofyorktown.com

This site's description of the Battle of Yorktown includes many little-known details and pictures:
www.britishbattles.com/battle-yorktown.htm

Here is more detailed information about the Battle of Yorktown:
www.patriotresource.com/battles/yorktown.html

Bibliography

Bonsal, Stephen. *When the French Were Here: A Narrative of the Sojourn of the French Forces in America, and Their Contribution to the Yorktown Campaign*. Garden City, NY: Doubleday, Doran, 1945.

Chidsey, Donald Barr. *Victory at Yorktown*. New York: Crown, 1962.

Decision at Yorktown, October, 1781: A French-American Victory. New York: French Embassy Press and Information Service, 1981.

Fleming, Thomas J. *Beat the Last Drum: The Siege of Yorktown, 1781*. New York: St. Martin's Press, 1963.

Grainger, John D. *The Battle of Yorktown, 1781: A Reassessment*. Woodbridge, England: Boydell Press, 2005.

Martin, Joseph Plumb. *Private Yankee Doodle: Being a Narrative of Some of the Adventures, Dangers and Sufferings of a Revolutionary Soldier*. Boston: Little, Brown, 1962.

Thacher, James. *Military Journal of the American Revolution*. Hartford, CT: Hurlbut, Williams, 1862.

Index

Page numbers in **boldface** are illustrations.

About the Author

Dennis Fradin is the author of 150 books, some of them written with his wife, Judith Bloom Fradin. Their book for Clarion, *The Power of One: Daisy Bates and the Little Rock Nine*, was named a Golden Kite Honor Book. Another of Dennis's well-known books is *Let It Begin Here! Lexington & Concord: First Battles of the American Revolution*, published by Walker. Other recent books by the Fradins include *Jane Addams: Champion of Democracy* for Clarion and *5,000 Miles to Freedom: Ellen and William Craft's Flight from Slavery* for National Geographic Children's Books. Their current project for National Geographic is the *Witness to Disaster* series about natural disasters. *Turning Points in U.S. History* is Dennis's first series for Marshall Cavendish Benchmark. The Fradins have three grown children and five grandchildren.